WPA ART

by Mary Evans

Harcourt

Orlando   Boston   Dallas   Chicago   San Diego

Visit The Learning Site!

www.harcourtschool.com

Have you ever seen a picture like this one?
This picture is so big, the painter had to use a
ladder to paint it!

Next time you're at a library or post office,
look at the walls. You may see mural paintings. If
you do, they were probably painted between
1935 and 1943.

A mural is a picture on a wall of a building. A
mural can also be on a ceiling. Murals are pictures
of many different subjects.

People have painted murals in all kinds of places. Prehistoric people painted pictures on the walls of their caves. The ancient Egyptians painted on the walls of their tombs. The Romans decorated their homes with murals.

In 1935 America was going through the Great Depression. Franklin D. Roosevelt was President. He started a program called the Works Progress Administration, also known as WPA. It was created to provide jobs for people who had no money.

The government supported painters, sculptors, writers, and musicians by paying them to make artwork, to write, and to perform for the community. All the artists enjoyed painting walls and other spaces that would not normally contain art. In this book, we look at some of the wonderful murals created during this time.

These murals are all over the country. You are most likely to find them in public buildings, such as schools and hospitals. By 1943, WPA artists had made 2,566 murals.

This mural is a picture of a county fair in Danbury, Connecticut. Usually, the fair took place in October. People who went to the fair could have fun going on exciting rides, playing games, and enjoying other attractions. They could also listen to an auctioneer asking audience members to bid on different items. The place where this fair was held is now a shopping center.

This mural shows a scene from American life. It is a typical example of the subjects WPA mural painters liked to paint.

What do you think the people in this mural are doing? This painting is about the Underground Railroad. Despite its name, it was not a railroad nor was it underground. In the mid-1800s, it was a system that helped slaves escape from their owners in the South. It was called "underground" because people worked on it in secret and "railroad" because it was so quick. Traveling north to freedom, the slaves often had to hide during the day. They clutched their belongings as they slowly moved northward.

They rested in places called "stations." The people that helped them along the way were called "conductors."

Notice that this painting is a night scene. How has the artist painted night? The dark colors make it look as if there is little light in the sky. Only the people around the lantern are lit by its bright, glowing fire.

Who is the "conductor" in this painting? Some figures on the far left have their backs toward us. Where do you think they are going?

Festival at Hamburg

This mural shows a city scene. It is called "Festival at Hamburg." It decorates the Hamburg Post Office in Hamburg, Iowa.

The bright colors in this painting give it a cheerful feeling. Everyone in the picture seems happy. People are dancing and holding hands. The weather is warm.

Notice the way the wide road in this picture looks as if it disappears into the distance. Painting the picture this way helps create depth. It also helps viewers imagine what might be beyond what is visible in the scene.

The people at the bottom of this picture are larger than the people at the top of it. Are the people at the bottom really bigger people? No, they're the same size.

The painter did this so that you would feel as though you were right there. Next time you're on a long street full of people, stand still at one end. Pretend you're looking at a painting on a flat surface. Do the people near you look the same size as the ones that are far away?

Men and Wheat

Work and workers were often subjects of WPA artists. This artist composed a powerful picture of farmers using what was modern machinery in the 1930s.

The tractor is pulling a reaper to cut his crop of ripe wheat. The reaper has a thresher attached to it. The heavy heads of golden wheat are shaken from the stem and poured into a bin.

Notice the strong vertical shaft of the thrasher in the very middle of the painting. It forms the top point of the triangle design the artist composed. Can you see the triangle of men, machines, and the wheat?

Apple Harvest

    This picture of an apple harvest hangs in the City Hall of Norwalk, Connecticut. Can you tell what time of year it is in this picture? What is the man on the ladder doing?

    If you look closely, you can learn something about apple harvesting from this mural. Can you tell what the steps for harvesting apples are? First, the apples are picked and put in baskets. What do you think the workers will do next?

Construction of a Dam

Construction of the Grand Coulee Dam on the Columbia River in the state of Washington was started in 1933. It took a long time and a tremendous amount of work to build. At one time, eight thousand men and women worked on the project. When it was completed in 1941, the dam was one mile long. At that time, it was the largest concrete structure in the world.

William Gropper painted this mural in 1939 for the Department of the Interior building in Washington, D.C. Today, the mural is on display at the Smithsonian Institution.

What three actions do you see? On the left, men are drilling rock to remove it. At the center, you see a crane carrying away a concrete form. On the right, men are building a framework to hold the form.

William Gropper did not waste any space. Look closely. Between the men drilling rock and the crane carrying the concrete form, the rising new dam glistens. Now look between the center figures and the men working on the right. You can see a concrete factory! The artist must have studied how dams are built before he painted his mural.

Murals often tell stories. What story does "Evening on the Farm" tell? The artist, Orr C. Fisher, seems to be telling us that everybody on the farm has a job to do. You learn more from a painting or mural if you ask yourself questions. Asking questions helps you notice details.

For example, why are the horses thirsty? Perhaps they galloped from a nearby farm. Maybe the person driving them was in a hurry. Where do you think the person on the horse in the background is coming from?

Evening on the Farm

Dredging for Oysters

In this painting, some men are working on an oyster boat. While the artist was painting this picture, men who worked on a real oyster boat watched him work.

What do you notice in this picture? The man stooping near the mast of the boat is wearing very tall boots. Do you know why he might wear these boots? Do the man in the blue coat and the man in the yellow coat look alike to you? They should. The artist used one man as a model for both of these men!

Painting people at work was popular among WPA artists. The man in this mural is drilling a big hole in a road. Can you describe the expression on his face? Explain how the artist made him look this way. Here are some hints: What kind of colors has the artist used? Where is the man looking? What can you tell from the way his mouth is painted?

We are all lucky to have a few of the WPA artworks left to admire. Many of the paintings made during this time no longer exist.